Verses From A
Flower Child

Lavita Lobo

Presentation by *BookLeaf Publishing*

Web: www.bookleafpub.com

E-mail: info@bookleafpub.com

ISBN: 9789363317499

First edition 2024

to my constants—my family.

Home, a Redefine

My home then, was confined to four walls
made of bricks, garnished with wall art,
furnished with cushions, soft and cosy

Not, no more!
My home is my Mother, whose endless love
is my most colourful palette

My home is my friend,
whose words soften my cold bruised heart

My home is my song, without which
I couldn't make sense of this chaos

My home is my soft heart, who takes troubles
with a large pinch of salt

Art, Not for My Present

Beating a dead horse and wandering away
Has always been good for my art
But terrible for my soul

Being somewhere, anywhere but here and now
Has always brought about a new song
But taken away a piece of my here and now

How do I compensate for the current loss of time
How to make it up to those who wait for me in
the now
While I wander away backwards, somewhere
far,
taking time to travel back while they wait for my
return

How terrible it is, to not be able to pause time
'Cause it waits for no one, not a single one
As the clock ticks, I make my choice

To stay here or drift away
Each bringing a gift and curse, which is only
mine to bear

To whoever says "life is perfect," get out of your
delusion; it's not even close
Just thank the philosophers who give you
pre-populated answer choices to calm the chaos,
but only for now

What About…

If you don't experience
What are you going to write about
If you don't feel
What are you going to sing about
If you don't dream
What are you going to live about
If you get it all
What are you going to be happy about
If you don't travel
What are you going to feel magical about
And if you don't love
What the hell are *you* about?

Never The Same

If you don't choose me now
The moment will pass
If you don't love me now
It'll never come back to the way it was

Be, Love

May you be kind
When no one else was
May you be Joy
When everything is gloomy
May you be the light
When everything seems dark
May you be the love
That every soul is looking for

Anything But War

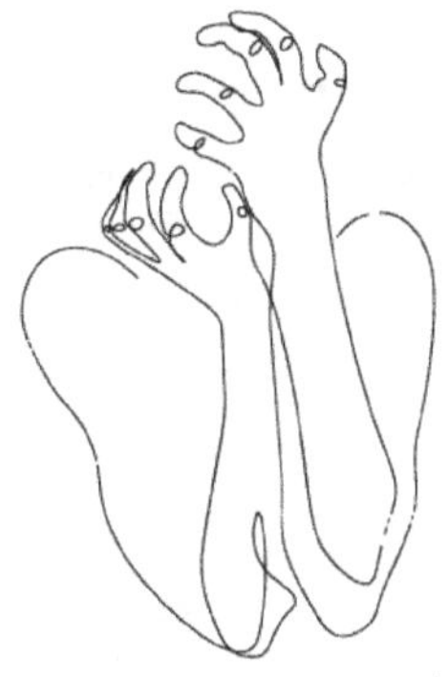

Make love, not war, they said
I say it's alright
Don't love, but don't make war either
Don't be nice, but don't make war
Don't even stay true, but please don't make war

Don't say the right things, but I beg, don't make
war
Don't accept, but, please, for the sake of
Humanity
Don't make war
- please

God's Child

No hate, no curse
You've bled love with every fibre
Stones pelted, wounds they hurt
Yet you didn't give up on your good heart

Dangerous, Peace

How dangerous I became
when I stopped justifying
Letting everyone imagine what they like
to each their own
to me, my own
How dangerously freeing that is
something not everyone feels
Being dangerous is a gift, a power
But with this power comes no responsibility
Only a lot of peace

A Short Story of Death:

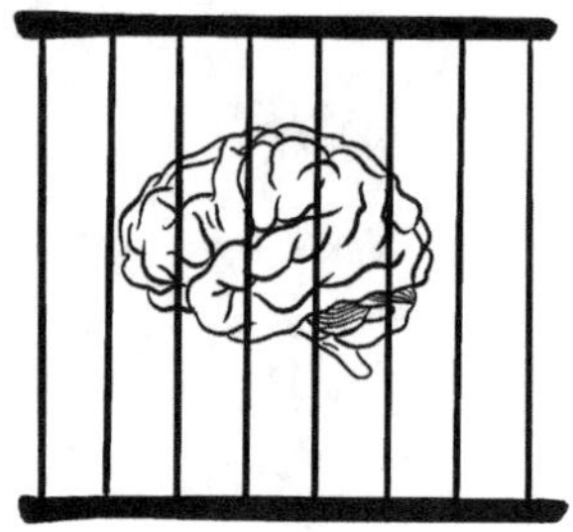

"Knock, knock"
Who's there?
"Possibility"
Ahh, no thank you
I'm comfortable

Prayer

11:11, years ago
You waited for your wish to come true
The thing that beings glimmer forever
11:11 in the present
You know you're the master of your fate
You are everything you prayed for

Hope, A Practice

If it's taking a while
use the while
to live some more

If it's not happening now
use the now
to build some more

If it's wanting to leave
use the space
to fill some more

and if it's wanting to just be
remember to open the doors
It's going to flow a lot more

Let it go

People leave
let them go
Eyes weep
let it flow
As they go,
There is more space
For things better than what were
Maybe, maybe not
But holding tight brings ache
In places you didn't know
So let it go, let it flow

Fill me up

The sound of nothing
Brings chatter to my head
The sound of music
a whole lot of tranquil
The sound of the breeze
a sense of quiet
and the sound of you
fills my entire being
- With love

Divine Plans

I planned it all
Big and small
How it should be,
Everything, overall
Took the steps,
Even missed a few
But every woman makes mistakes
Everyone, even me and you
But then, I walked
Through an open door
Unplanned, unannounced
Saw some wildflowers
Blooming for but themselves
And anyone who wants to stay a while
I stayed a while, some more,
A bit longer, just a little bit more?
And in that moment I realised
I'm not made for the plan,
I'm made for the flow of the Divine

Shallow Being

They said wealth is the only way
To get people to respect you
Respected by whom?
The ones who only respect the wealthy?
Oh my love, but they fade away with your
money
The ones left are the kind souls
Who know respect as a virtue
And not something born of convenience
For those are the ones
You need to keep, and keep close
The rest can wear their dresses so pretty
and flaunt the shallow end of their being

You've Changed

I saw you up close
I knew something had changed
Your smile wasn't as full as it used to be
I wanna ask, "Who hurt you this time?"
'Cause it's always someone who snatches the
light
from your eyes
So who is it? I'm curious but I don't ask
I see you trying and I don't want to open the
wound

There's a stone-cold heart
Where there used to be care
There's a teary stare
Where there used to be soft glares
There are calculated moves
Where hugs free-flowed

There's a pause before your words
Where sweetness always flowed

So who was it?
I finally ask as I look into the mirror
And I say, "It was me all along, boundary-less."

Becoming, You

Let it down, your hair
But never your gaze
Let it go, your inhibitions
But never your freedom
Let it free, your words
But never your values
Let it out, your thoughts
But never your self-worth
Let yourself be what you want to be
Someone today, someone else tomorrow
Till you find your amalgamation of personalities
That truly blend into the absolute YOU

I'm Beauty

Today I am jazz
Tomorrow I'm the blues
Yesterday I was the dancing Bollywood
I hope every day I'm a song
One that remembers to hit the play button
Because with art, everything is beauty—
Your pain, your happiness, your hurt, your
longing
Let it all be a song
while you sway to every note, of every feeling

Love, The Whole

I wanted the world,
The highs, the lows,
the glitter and gold

But then, I didn't have love

Now that I do have love
I want nothing but the serene,the mundane,
the little things

Now that I have love,it fills me,
It fulfils me,it takes a lot of space
It demands nothing but my presence
Now that I have love

I'm Whole

For, The Ocean

If not for the ocean
I wouldn't see the infinite
If not for the ocean
I wouldn't welcome the daylight
In the most perfect way
If not for the ocean
I wouldn't know timelessness

If not for the ocean
I wouldn't watch the moon
in twice its glory—
One in the sky, and one in the sea

If not for the ocean
I wouldn't know quiet
In the extreme sound of the breeze

If not for the ocean,
I wouldn't believe
There are more miracles to be found,
more mysteries, more of it all, more of me

Undoing, Life

Most of life
Goes in undoing—
For everything we were taught
to become an adult
They couldn't be further
from what we truly need

Some time in the sun,
Some time for play,
Some time for fun,
and only
Some time for serious learning

Some moments of cry,
Some moments of jealousy,
Some moments to scream,
Some moments to be messy

All this suppressed
To be the perfect, poised person
the society needs

Couldn't be far
From what we were truly meant to
Be.

Lovers

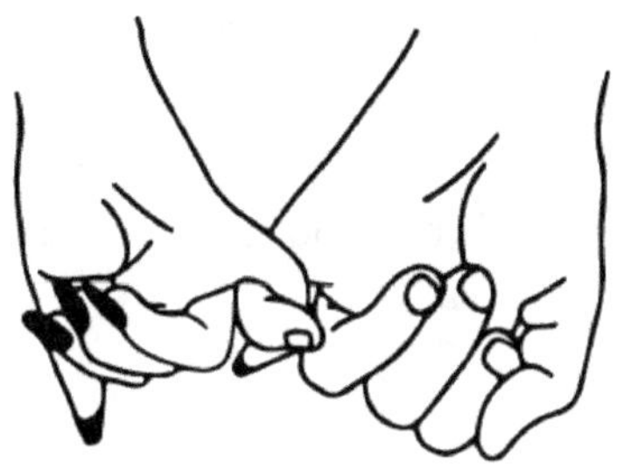

Lovers are tough
Waking up each day choosing to consider
someone else's needs
In this ever-confused world
Where selfishness is mistaken for self-care

Lovers bring softness
In a world made to harden and build walls, many
and mighty

Lovers are brave
To be hurting, yet choosing
To forgive

Yes, loving can hurt
But not loving is a life not lived

Not loving is like having tons of wealth
But choosing to live miserably

Not loving is a box of gifts, unopened

Not loving is a Mustang perpetually put away in
a dusty garage

We are made to break and mend; we are made to
choose love *over and over again.*

The gift of today

Today is the day I decide
To let my hair down
(Flow)
To breathe consciously
(Rhythm)
To pause and reflect
(Patience)
To dance to my favourite tune
(Move)
To take that long drive
(Self-love)
To make that call
(Courage)

Today is the day
I become summer's favourite flower
Autumn's favourite leaf
Spring's freshest air
And winter's most precious daylight

Anti-Capitalist

Here's to slowing down
Here's to reading more
Here's to listening mindfully
Here's to bean bags and warm teas
Here's to breathing deep and eating clean
Here's to more of me
Less of the noisy world
Here's to healing slowly, but surely

Light as feather

Somewhere between chaos and finding peace
I left a part of me
An invisible thread still binds me to it
But it grows thinner every passing year
The pull gets lighter and I get freer

The feeling of being so light
It's new and unfamiliar
I feel like holding on to that thread
That binds me to the part I left behind
But the cost of it is I won't be able to fly

But fly I must
The flight is my destiny
The clouds are calling
A pathway to heaven

some days, don't try

Some days there's just no winning
No matter how hard you try
So take that endless nap
Have that treat
Binge-watch that show
Laze to your heart's content
But make sure tomorrow is the best day you've
ever had..

From my darkest places
Has come my deepest wisdom—
One I wouldn't know of,
If not for the void in my heart.
The emptiness made space for so much joy
Just like a freshly filled air balloon ready to fly.

So fear not the dark
Live there a while, if you like.
For someday, you will crave the light
And after that, there will be only sunflowers for
a while

You are made to be resilient, my friend
It's what's always been in your blood
So fear not the dark
Befriend it, like the night jasmine—
It's always the better choice.

Inwards

I am the magic in my own plan
All I need, is a recipe for self-belief

Vicious loop

I live in the past
I think of my future
I have no time for the present
Therefore I suffer

My prayer, for you

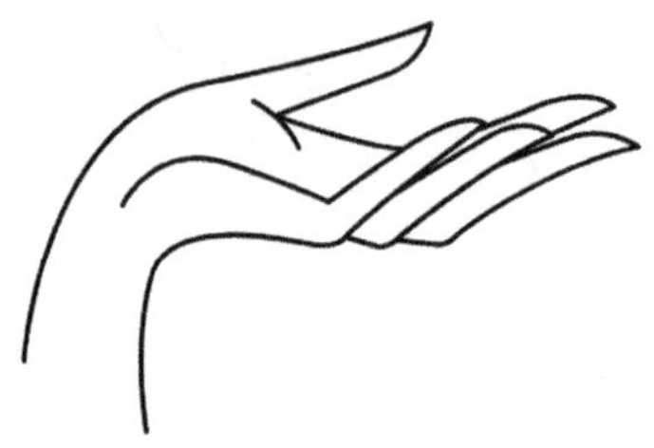

How long have you been unconscious?
How long have you been sleeping
You're empty, it looks like; are you still seeking?

I see you, I see you
I really see you
I wish you saw yourself the way I do

If only you could see yourself through me
You'd see the emptiness like a canvas
All ready for colour

But that's my vision, not yours
My control would be a lost cause

I pray, when you hit the bottom
You bounce back with speed
Like a luminous shooting star
The onlookers see
And wish for themselves
To have your spark

The idea of you

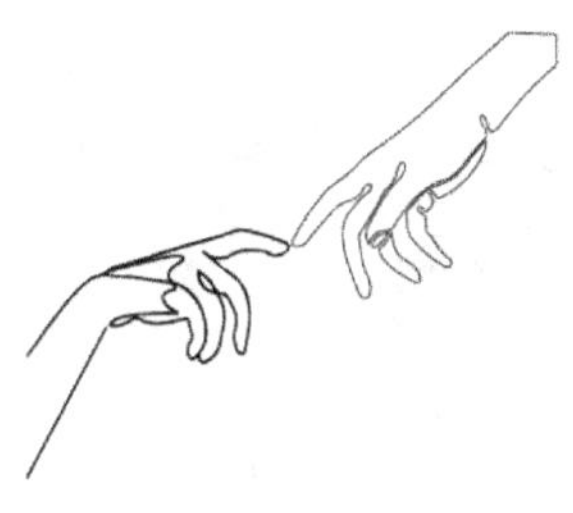

You're my daydream
You're my nightmare
Afraid to lose you, if you're mine
Afraid of the future without your sight
I think I like this little game
'Cause you're perfect in my mind
Mysterious, divine, fresh, and fine
Maybe I won't find you perfect when you're
mine
So stay where you are
While I live with my imaginary perception
'Cause I like this little dream
My own creation
Makes for a song,
Makes for a poetic ideation

Dilemma

I wonder if you're my forever
My perfect person
I wonder if I'm meant to love you
Or you're just a lesson
I wonder if I should live like there's no
tomorrow
Or live cautiously—I don't know
My heart says *yes*
My past says *no*

I decide on the now
But what if the heart breaks? It's inevitable
It'll mend if broken
And you will learn your lesson

You were not made to preserve your love
You were not made for perfection
You were made to break, rebuild, receive, and
give

You were made to feel it all
You were made to live

A woman's plea

Her life is a poetry
She's here to move you
A muse to artists
Enamoured by her being
A force of nature, a mother, a lover
Imperfect, yet so perfect
A life giver,
And yet all she asks
Is for "basic respect"

Embracing the curse of depth

To feel so deeply
Is often categorised as a curse
But that curse, my dear
Is the one that will show you beauty
That curse breathes life

Embrace it, that darn curse
Like a witch and her witchcraft
And watch the magic of being alive
Sprinkle all around like fairy dust

Poof.. there you are
A breathing and living soul
Experiencing everything
So deeply, just the way
It was meant to be

So hug it tight
For as long as you feel
You will live to tell stories
Like no one ever will

Paradox

have you ever been so happy
that it makes your heart sink a bit
in sadness?

have you ever been so sad
that you start laughing at your misery?

have you ever been so in love
that it makes you hate a little?

have you ever gotten so angry
that you discover a softness in you?

I'm for sure
a walking-talking paradox
And you?

Getting it off my chest

There's something so negative
about people who are so positive

There I said it!

No Hurry Today

I wake up to the sound of raindrops
Almost drum-like over the roof,
And on the window pane;
Gloomy and cold
I'm in no hurry today.

While I sip my tea of herbs and spices;
Looking out at the lush green,
Something changes in me.
A sense of tranquil while I breathe
I'm in no hurry today

I pull out my favourite music
It sets the perfect mood
The ambience and the nature outside
Calls for the perfect song,
I'm in no hurry today

You, and me

A bench for two
A pot of tea
An open window
Lots to see
Conversation flows
Like the breeze
While I pour some
For you and me
Deeper breaths
A beautiful flow
Mind it's shut
Heart it opens
Wearing it on my sleeve
Ready to run and latch on to yours
Synchronised thoughts
Inhibitions dropped
All that remains
Is a pot of tea,
And you, and me

Delulu..

Reality, my friend
Is only heart-breaking
Some delusion and a ton of hope
Is the way to your destiny

Worthwhile

My heart skips a beat..

When I see the twinkling night sky
When I see chemtrails of white
When I see a newborn's smile
When I catch a rainbow's sight

My heart skips a beat..
When I think of you and I

For you, my love

You're an emotion
That can only be expressed through a song

Everything has its time,

Wait.

* 9 7 8 9 3 6 3 3 1 7 4 9 9 *